Flowers

VIOLETS

John F. Prevost
ABDO & Daughters

Published by Abdo & Daughters, 4940 Viking Drive, Suite 622, Edina, Minnesota 55435.

Copyright © 1996 by Abdo Consulting Group, Inc., Pentagon Tower, P.O. Box 36036, Minneapolis, Minnesota 55435 USA. International copyrights reserved in all countries. No part of this book may be reproduced in any form without written permission from the publisher.

Printed in the United States.

Cover Photo credits: Peter Arnold, Inc.
Interior Photo credits: Peter Arnold, Inc.

Edited by Bob Italia

Library of Congress Cataloging-in-Publication Data

Prevost, John F.
      Violets / John F. Prevost.
      p. cm. -- (Flowers)
      Includes index.
      Summary: Describes the structure of and growing conditions for violets,
      with information about the various species and the pests and diseases that may affect
      them.
      ISBN 1-56239-613-7
      1. Violets--Juvenile literature. [1. Violets.] I. Title. II. Series: Prevost, John F.
      Flowers
      QK495.V5P74 1996
      583' .135--dc20   96-10482
                                                        CIP
                                                        AC

Contents

Violets and Family

Violets are a group of small flowering plants. Most are yellow and blue. White and pink are also common colors. Often, three colors mix on one flower. Violets grow in lawns, planters, and gardens.

There are more than 600 kinds of plants, shrubs, and vines in the violet family. The most popular wild violets are the Johnny Jump Up (or wild pansy), birdfoot violet, and the downy yellow violet. Many are found in woodlands and **marshy** areas.

Opposite page:
The birdfoot violet.

Roots, Soil, and Water

Violets pull water and **nutrients** from the soil with their thin roots that also keep the plants from falling over. A few violets have thick **taproots** that help the plants store food for the next year.

Some violets are only found in rocky, mountain soil. Others grow only in wet, **acid** soils.

Most violets like moist soil. If the violets are not planted in the right soil, they will die. The soil must be fertile. Without enough food, the violet will not grow or flower.

Many wild violets grow in special soil conditions.

Stems, Leaves, and Sunlight

Sunlight is important to every green plant. Plants use sunlight to change water, **nutrients,** and air into food and **oxygen**. This process is called **photosynthesis**.

The stems hold up the leaves and allow them to collect sunlight. Stems send water from the roots to the leaves where food is made. The food then returns to the roots.

Violet leaves are round, heart- or kidney-shaped. Some **varieties** have yellow or purple leaves. Most have green leaves.

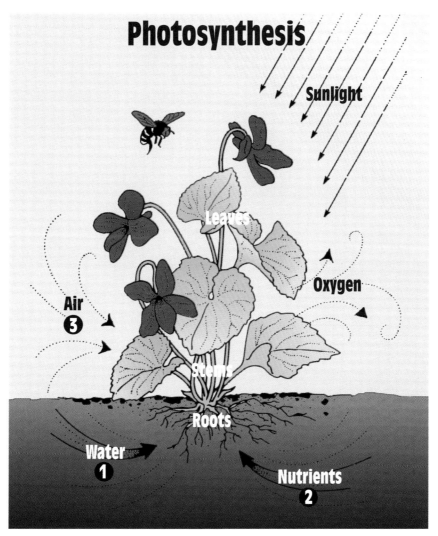

Photosynthesis

Sunlight

Leaves

Oxygen

Air 3

Stems

Roots

Water 1

Nutrients 2

Ground water (1) and nutrients (2) travel through the roots and stems and into the leaves where air (3) is drawn in. Then the plant uses sunlight to change these three elements into food and oxygen.

Flowers

Violets are often raised for their small flowers, which are 1/2 inch (1 cm) to 4 inches (10 cm) across. Most are yellow or blue and have a sweet smell.

There are three main parts to a violet's flower: the **petal**, the **stamen**, and the **pistil**. The petals are the showy part of the flower. The stamen contains **pollen,** which **fertilizes** the pistil's **ovules**. The ovules grow into seeds.

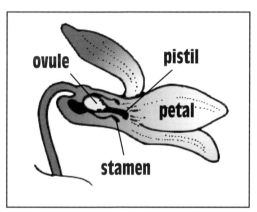

The stamen fertilizes the pistil's ovules which grow into seeds.

Seeds

Violet seeds grow in small **capsules** that form where the **petals** grow before they fall off. When the capsules are ripe, they pop open and toss the seeds away from the parent plant.

Seeds form when **pollen fertilizes ovules** inside the **pistil**. The ovules then grow into seeds.

Inside the seeds are the plant **embryos.** Each seed contains plant food. Most seeds need a **dormant** period before they will grow.

Violets have other ways to **reproduce.** Some have **runners** that grow roots when they touch the ground. Other plants send up new leaf growth from spreading roots.

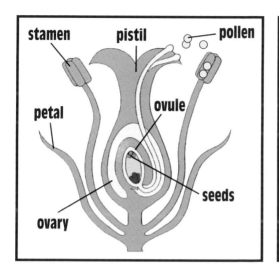

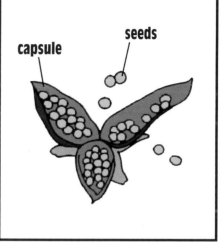

As the pistil's ovules grow into seeds, the ovary forms a capsule. The capsule protects the seeds until they are ripe. Each seed contains a tiny plant embryo which will one day grow into a violet plant.

Insects and Other Friends

Violets grow flowers to attract insects. The flowers' color and smell invites flying insects to land on the **bloom.** The flowers also attract ants and other crawling insects. Some flowers make **nectar** to reward the insects with a small meal.

Insects help the flower **reproduce** by carrying **pollen** from plant to plant. Many **predators** live on violets. Spiders eat insects that may attack the violet.

Many types of bugs live on flowers.

Pests and Diseases

Violets have little trouble with insect **pests**. But sometimes **aphids** are a problem. They feed on the sap of the violet plant. Aphids are easily controlled with **predatory** insects or **poison.**

Ladybugs and other predatory insects eat aphids.

Slugs and snails are bigger problems. Frogs, toads, and birds can help control them. Removing their hiding places or using poisoned baits also works.

Diseases will attack violets that are not planted in the right locations or are damaged during planting.

*Healthy violets have little trouble
with diseases and pests.*

Varieties

There are more than 600 kinds of violets. Many are grown in gardens and yards.

The most common **varieties** are pansies, violas, and violettas. They are grown for their flowers' size and color.

Other kinds of violets are often called wildflowers. Small blue violet, Nuttall's violet, and the Canadian violet are just a few that grow in North America.

Opposite page: The Canadian violet.

Violets and the Plant Kingdom

The plant kingdom is divided into several groups, including flowering plants, fungi, plants with bare seeds, and ferns.

 Flowering plants grow flowers to make seeds. These seeds often grow inside protective ovaries or fruit.

 Fungi are plants without leaves, flowers, or green coloring, and cannot make their own food. They include mushrooms, molds, and yeast.

 Plants with bare seeds (such as evergreens and conifers) do not grow flowers. Their seeds grow unprotected, often on the scale of a cone.

 Ferns are plants with roots, stems, and leaves. They do not grow flowers or seeds.

There are two groups of flowering plants: monocots (MAH-no-cots) and dicots (DIE-cots). Monocots have seedlings with one leaf. Dicots have seedlings with two leaves.

The violet family is one type of dicot.

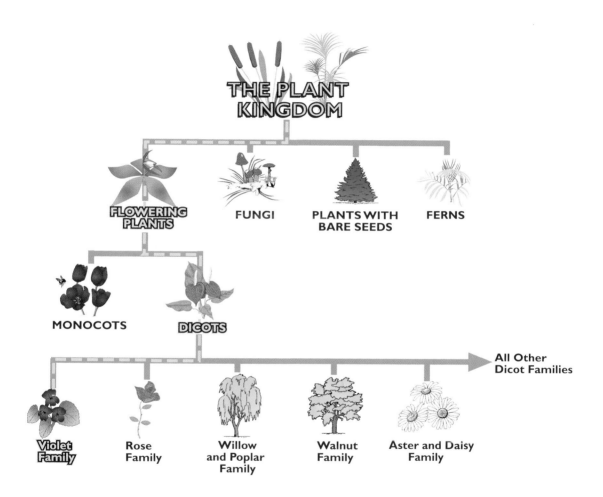

THE PLANT KINGDOM

FLOWERING PLANTS

FUNGI

PLANTS WITH BARE SEEDS

FERNS

MONOCOTS

DICOTS

All Other Dicot Families

Violet Family

Rose Family

Willow and Poplar Family

Walnut Family

Aster and Daisy Family

Glossary

acid - A chemical substance that helps form a salt.

aphid (AY-fid) - A small insect that sucks sap from a plant.

bloom - To have flowers; also, a flower blossom.

capsule - A tiny container.

disease (diz-EEZ) - A sickness.

dormant (DOOR-mant) - The state of rest or inactivity.

embryo (EM-bree-oh) - An early stage of plant growth, before sprouting from a seed.

fertilize (FUR-tuh-lies) - To develop the ovule into a seed.

marsh - Low land covered at times by water.

nectar - A sweet fluid found in some flowers.

nutrients (NEW-tree-ents) - Substances that help a plant grow and stay healthy.

ovules (AH-vules) - A seed before it is fertilized by pollen.

oxygen (OX-ih-jen) - A gas without color, taste, or odor found in air and water.

pest - A harmful or destructive insect.

petal (PET-ull) - One of several leaves that protect the center of a flower.

photosynthesis (foe-toe-SIN-thuh-sis) - The use of sunlight to make food.

pistil (PIS-till) - The female (seed-making) flower part.

poison - A substance that is dangerous to life or health.

pollen (PAH-lin) - A yellow powder that fertilizes flowers.

pollinate (PAH-lih-nate) - The use of pollen to fertilize a flower.

predator (PRED-uh-tore) - An animal that eats other animals.

reproduce - To produce offspring.

runner - A slender stem that takes root along the ground, thus making new plants.

stamen (STAY-men) - The male flower part (the flower part that makes pollen).

taproot - A main root with smaller side roots.

varieties (vuh-RYE-uh-tees) - Different types of plants that are closely related.

Index